HOROSCOPE

2024

LEO

Angeline A. Rubi

Alina Rubi

Published Independently

All rights reserved © 2024.

Astrologers: Alina A. Rubi and Angeline Rubi

Editing: Angeline. Rubi

rubiediciones29@gmail.com

Who is Leo?

Dates: July 24th - August 23rd

Day: Sunday

Color: Yellow, gold

Element: Fire

Compatibility: Aquarius, Sagittarius, Aries,

Symbol:

Fixed Mode

Polarity: Male

Ruling planet: Sun

House 5

Metal: Gold.

Quartz: Ruby, diamonds, Onyx.

Constellation: Leo

Leo Personality

His personality is simply exuberant. Ruled by the Sun, he possesses a force that motivates others to move and always wants to shine and dominate.

This quality can become a defect because he can be quite dominant. He does not know revenge, is generous materially and personally, and is the best boss for a group.

This sign is enthusiastic, creative, and often sympathetic to the circumstances of others; they love luxury and adventure; taking risks motivates them.

They are also characterized by having a high concept of everything, especially of themselves, that is why they flee from vulgarity.

They are organized, often excel in positions of responsibility, and have a great ability to get the equipment that allows them to develop their objectives. Obstacles do not prevent them from moving forward. In fact, they grow with them.

They are loyal and protective. They are excellent friends, affectionate and protective. They do not fail their loved ones and that makes that, from time to time, they are involved in other people's problems.

They are bad losers: they are quite ambitious and defiant and like to show off. If something doesn't go their way, they react destructively.

They make the most of every second, love life, love to have fun and enjoy all kinds of entertainment: music, cinema, theater, nature. If they can't enjoy their hobbies, their mood changes and they shut down.

They are in love; it is a feeling that they love, and it is one of the fundamental ingredients of that sauce of life that they are always looking for. With their partner they like to feel admired and praised.

Elegant from the cradle, have you noticed how they walk and how they move? In general, Leo natives have a striking physique, they walk in an elegant way, and they usually have captivating looks.

Proud and haughty, they can be tyrannical and, at times, somewhat despot-like.

Leo Horoscope

General

2024 brings energies of second chances for Leo's, so consider what this could mean for you.

There can be big changes in your relationships, the way you approach and handle them, the people you attract, and what you want and need in your personal relationships.

Lunar Eclipses bring an intense focus on what you need to transform to improve your relationships. You may have to deal with something you have been running away from for some time, and this can be upsetting, but will ultimately help you move forward.

You can feel more ambitious and strive for success. You will achieve some kind of success that has been years in the making.

You will feel excited about the work you are doing, and if you lack passion for it, this year you can focus on trying to find a new job.

The new Moons will give you the opportunity to look for a new job, if that's what you want, and you can start new projects and focus on what you are excited about doing.

You may need to make some major changes, but you need to be smart about it. If you love what you do, you can make great strides and succeed. Opportunities may arise that will help you invest, and you'll find creative ways to feel more confident in the way you invest your money.

You must protect your health, don't try to do everything at once. Deal with issues as they arise.

The times when you will come face to face with strong challenges are the beginning of the year and the summer months.

Love
Pluto has been in your area of love for over a decade, so you have been more serious and intense about love and take it much more seriously. What love is, and means to you, has undergone a transformation, but you now feel more aligned with what is true for you. You know what you really want and need in a

relationship and if you are committed you are willing to give.

During Mercury retrograde periods existing problems in your love relationships will increase and this can make you feel frustrated and impatient with others, but you need to work on all these problems and improve.

This year can be a good time to rekindle the flames of an existing relationship or reconnect with an old love, especially with the new Moons that can provide opportunities to do so. Either way, you should try to nurture your connections with others and give them support.

Saturn and Neptune will be in your sector of intimacy all year, and for that reason having a spiritual connection is important to you with those you are closest to. You will be more assertive and realistic in dealing with your emotional ties to others.

You can focus on old problems and traumas that have gotten in the way of these bonds in a healthy way and learn lessons about the past that will help you create better bonds in the future.

For some Leo's, love could lead to marriage. If you are a single Leo, be prepared to find your true love. But be careful, you should not trust everyone because some people who might try to take advantage of your kindness.

Married Leo's will see happiness and growth in their families. To keep your partner happy, focus on their well-being. This year, you will write incredible memories with your partner. Your love will grow stronger, reaching new horizons.

Misunderstandings may arise from time to time, so during difficult times, it is important to be patient. Remember to respect your partner's decisions and not force your opinions. With patience, you will keep your relationship strong and happy.

Some Leo could reconnect with a past love, so keep your heart open. You will be able to clear up old misunderstandings and enjoy love.

You will cherish every moment, and your family relationships will be strengthened with love and understanding.

Economy

Uranus joins Jupiter until May 25 in your area of money. This combo is fabulous for making sudden progress and experiencing success in a quick, unexpected, and unconventional way. You can approach your long-term goals and plans in a new way, and this will open more doors for you.

2024 will be a mix of gains and losses. Your hard work will bring you money, but family and other problems will cause financial instability. Try to save money for when difficult situations arise. Spending wisely can save you some headaches.

The first half of the year you will have a mix of good and challenging times as your expenses will increase, but you will also earn more money. If you don't control your expenses, you could face financial problems.

Anyway, thanks to Jupiter, if you set your mind to it, you will be able to save money as resources will come to you from different sources and you will be able to buy a house, if that is something you have been wishing for.

If you don't have health insurance, health care costs can hurt your finances. That's why you need to watch your spending and be smart with your money. Remember to make wise financial decisions.

Leo Health

You will be in fantastic health this year. You will feel energetic, happy, and strong, both in body, mind, and soul. Being mentally strong is important, and luckily you will start the year with a strong mentality. Feeling healthy will help you succeed in your work.

You will be healthy and disease-free. If you have any chronic health problems, this could be the year to overcome them. To stay healthy, try adding meditation and exercise to your daily routine. Don't forget that keeping your mind calm and stress-free is key to staying healthy.

Rest is important for good health; you should drink plenty of water and expose yourself to sunlight to obtain vitamin D.

Adult Leos may experience knee or joint pain, specifically during the winter season.

Change your eating habits for better health. Be careful with accidents and injuries, especially when driving or playing sports.

Family

You will be focused on home and family matters. You will work to finish projects at home, and this will help you feel more comfortable, stable, and emotionally secure.

During Full Moon periods family problems may surface, it is important to address and resolve them.

The family environment will be very calm and harmonious in general during the year. Any problems that arise will be resolved amicably. There may be health problems with adult family members that require medical attention.

Professional obligations may take you away from your family members, but there will be celebrations and the addition of new family members.

Occasional breakups with your partner may occur due to family disagreements. Be very careful when dealing with your siblings, as they may have legal problems due to inheritances or legacies. Do not act hastily.

You may be able to establish a stable relationship if you are single, in general there are numerous opportunities to improve your love relationships.

Important Dates
March 25 *- Lunar Eclipse in Leo (Full Moon)*

This Eclipse will put an end to attitudes that hurt you. You should try to put limits on people who have crossed your path. There is a possibility that you will end a toxic relationship, and it will be for your own good.

July 2 *- Mercury enters Leo.*

July 11 *- Venus enters Leo. This transit will impact your romantic relationships and the way you relate to others. You may also become more dramatic and demanding in relationships, so be very careful.*

July 22nd - *The Sun enters Leo. Happy Return of the Sun.*

08/04/2024 New Moon in Leo. *During this period, you will be enthusiastic, excited, and ready for action. Opportunities may come your way. You should take initiatives and go for what you want, and make things happen. This New Moon arrives a few days before Mercury retrograde in your sign, so you may be more focused on a second chance.*

8/14/2024 to 8/28/2024 Mercury retrogrades in Leo *(after beginning in Virgo). This can cause a lot of misunderstandings, lack of focus, and you may feel that little things keep popping up and demanding your attention. You may be scattered, anxious and stressed. Try to have some healthy stress management strategies in place before the retrograde begins so you can handle it well and it will be easy.*

November 4 - *Mars enters Leo. Mars in your sign is traditionally a time of great energy and enthusiasm for new beginnings and business. You will be excited about the opportunities you have. Take advantage of this early because Mars will be retrograde starting*

December 6 in your sign, and ends the year retrograde in Leo. This can amplify your frustrations, and annoyances, something that can easily irritate you and make you explode. You may have small accidents as a result.

November 18, 19- *Leonid meteor shower in Leo. Meteor showers represent times of transition. This is an excellent opportunity to show the world how you want to be seen. You could plan a trip or resume friendships from the past. This meteor shower represents a time of faith and trust.*

Leo Monthly Horoscopes 2024

January 2024

Leo, this month you may find love while you are still on vacation. If this is not the case, you may meet your better half at school or work.

Your charisma will make you experience enviable encounters and eroticism will take over your life. Unfortunately, when everything seems to be fine, the phantom of jealousy will silently approach and afflict you with the most unrealistic fears.

The more equanimous Leo will discard their doubts. There will be nothing new at work, everything will follow its rhythm and there will be no specific changes.

After the 23rd you must be very patient and be careful in the way you communicate, it is important that you do not make promises that you cannot keep. Try to express your emotions correctly, even if you are not satisfied.

At work you will have excellent performance and productivity, however, it is advisable that you concentrate on completing pending tasks,

Success will be present in your life, but you should not overestimate its impact and get involved in any investment or large purchase. If that happens, you run the risk of losing financial liquidity.

Leo should trust his intuition when looking for sources of income.

January is a good time to conceive a child.

Lucky numbers
6 - 10 - 12 - 14 - 31

February 2024

In this month of love, you will be enthusiastic and will want to do more than one thing at a time. Do not make any decision without thinking, if you act on impulse everything will go wrong. You will be involved in turbulent situations.

Those who have a partner will experience satisfactory days in the sexual area. Eroticism will characterize every encounter for singles, so it is advisable to avoid ambivalent situations.

Be careful with your family when traveling, especially when it is raining because there is danger of accidents.

Some breakdowns can happen to household appliances in your home.

Be very careful when communicating. You must use the right tone even in text messages and emails. but if it is the only avenue available to you, use it to your advantage. You should try to maintain as much good humor in your communications as possible.

Lucky numbers
2 - 24 - 28 - 29 - 31

March 2024

You will experience linear emotions this month, feeling confused in the head, nervous in the heart and with exaggerated feelings.

You will need a lot of prudence in love, and patience with your work colleagues to get through this difficult period.

If you have many projects and ideas underway, you must remember that everything comes to fruition over time. Instead of rushing, what you should do is to take the opportunity to perfect your projects.

In the area of finances, you will not be immune to unnecessary expenses that will sabotage your budget. Try to be prudent.

Despite controversies with your colleagues and superiors, you will achieve your objectives and obtain important material improvements. Those who work independently will have the support of destiny to succeed in everything they start and will be able to increase their purchasing power.

At the end of the month let life surprise you and enjoy the pleasures it offers you, remember that not only work is important, but you should also have fun and spend time with your friends.

Lucky numbers
3 - 6 - 11 - 19 - 21

April 2024

This month love will be very good, if you are starting to get to know someone you will probably feel very connected, you just must be patient.

Family will take a back seat this month, but you won't feel guilty like other times.

Do not stop meeting that person who will suddenly appear in your life, even if you feel fear, it is important not to confuse this feeling of uncertainty with fear. What you have are doubts, related to bad experiences you had in the past. You must give love a chance.

Watch your health carefully. The hurried pace of life can force you to ignore certain recurring illnesses, which can lead to unfortunate consequences. You must have a rational balance between work and rest. You should have a hobby, buy long-desired things, meet with friends, or spend time with your family.

At the end of the month, you will have to make important decisions about your future career. If you do not have a job, you will have to analyze some options that do not look favorable in this period.

Lucky numbers

9 - 10 - 16 - 20 - 31

May 2024

A person you know a lot is having feelings about you. This change of attitude is the symptom that he or she is interested in you.

There are many things going on in your home that you may not know about.

A business trip may be waiting for you at the end of the month.

You should not invest in property or buy cars; these types of purchases can cause problems. It will involve more expenses than you expected at the beginning.

Single Leo's will be looking for a partner, remember that a first impression and interesting topics of conversation are important. It is best that they act without haste to avoid ruining a satisfactory relationship.

You work with many people, and sometimes some are unbearable. Don't let this affect you, begin to accept the mistakes of others, just as they accept yours. You will have a confrontation with someone at work, don't let the relationship break up.

Lucky numbers
7 - 8 - 16 - 22 - 31

June 2024

This month do not let past mistakes prevent you from loving again, you must take that big step with that person you are getting to know. Do not allow other people to get involved in your relationship.

You will start this month struggling with your bad mood, and you will feel very pressured and confused. Instead of running around you should take a break. Use this time to think about what you want to do. In the financial area you will have some ups and downs that will be difficult to handle unless you are organized with your expenses.

You need to make changes in the way you are doing your work, you are having a hard time doing certain things, especially if it involves technology.

However, by the end of the month you will be very enthusiastic and excel in everything you do. This may cause people to envy your success.

This month you will have problems related to the digestive system, so focus on a healthy and balanced diet, try to get plenty of rest. Try to find peace and your own harmony.

Lucky numbers
5 - 9 - 13 - 20 - 26

July 2024

This is not a good month to start romances, and those who have established relationships the situation will be critical. You must make smart decisions in love, if you have been dating someone for some time and that person has everything you need to be happy, do not be afraid to establish a serious commitment.

You should review your diet. Walk outdoors and exercise frequently. You must lose the fear of ending toxic relationships because you must take control of your life. It is time to start abandoning bad habits.

The restrictions you are putting on your life and the lives of your family members, you should let them go. You don't have to influence other people's lives all the time. If someone is doing something that is not right, advise him or her, but do not decide for that person.

Before making important investment decisions, you should talk to your loved ones. Your family will help you achieve success. Listen to their ideas. Proper financial planning combined with rational spending will result in the financial stability you need.

Lucky numbers
18 - 20 - 25 - 28 - 32

August 2024

During this month remember that you should not carry other people's blames, even if it is your partner or parents. Everyone should be responsible for their own growth.

You must be clear about what you want if you are going to approach that person you are attracted to because this person is someone who does not accept games and wants to form a couple for life. He or she is probably your soul mate.

You can't generate more money if you don't invest. You've been too comfortable in your comfort zone, but you must take a leap of faith.

At the end of the month certain obstacles will sabotage your plans with delays and lack of communication. There is the possibility of traveling abroad, both for fun and for business. Remember not to miss the opportunity to renew yourself in your professional area, do not pretend to succeed with the same knowledge you acquired in your studies, it is good to keep learning. You should take advanced courses, learn new technologies and learn how to use them.

Lucky numbers
9 - 13 - 21 - 22 - 27

September 2024

This month there are planetary aspects that will affect your profession. An unscrupulous person will cause you to fall behind on a project.

If you don't have a partner, you should think about going out with friends and socializing because love literally lies in your path. Remember that even though there is chaos everywhere, it doesn't have to affect you. Try not to let other people's problems be your problems. Try to be close enough to observe, but far enough away to keep your hands clean.

This month you will have the need to call someone to apologize for a mistake you made, it could be an ex-partner.

You are beginning a key stage in your life; it is time to start thinking about the steps you must take to achieve everything you have set out to do.

Your actions at the end of the month will yield the results you have desired. Things will return to normal. If, by chance, a project is delayed, don't try to rush it, take the opportunity to structure it a little more, because the delay is a sign that you should take care of details that you have been ignoring.

Lucky numbers
5 - 6 - 26 - 31 - 33

October 2024

This month you will find yourself in situations that will arouse very strong emotions that you will not be able to deal with. You will take everything personally.

Financially it is advisable not to make too many large purchases. Try to keep your expenses under control.

You will be able to reach beneficial agreements with your superiors, although you will see the results in time. You must be very careful with your reactions.

You should start taking more care of your health, it is likely that you have some condition, do not get discouraged if any medical result does not go as expected, you can turn this situation around later.

You will be confronted with someone who has a lot of influence in your work, you can't let them walk all over you, if you let them, it will always be like that.

Some family conflicts will embitter your life at the end of the month, it is advisable that you leave the problems aside and do not allow the difference you have had to get bigger.

Lucky numbers
4 - 5 - 18 - 20 - 32

November 2024

This month you will put aside many things you like and give priority to work to earn more money. Do not stop practicing exercise as it brings great benefits to your health and your mood. You should also leave room for fun, not always everything should be work, you should start to enjoy more.

You will have very little patience with the people you work with, and this will cause you discomfort to the point of wanting to leave your job and look for other options. Friction is normal, especially when we share with the same people every day. You should not leave the place where you are because it is likely that you will not find something with the same conditions.

It is not a good idea to complain to your partner about everything. Love is an investment. The money, time, and effort we invest is transformed into the well-being of the person we love.

You may want to partner with someone you don't know to start a business. You must formulate your strategies wisely.

Lucky numbers
3 - 25 - 28 - 34 - 36

December 2024

Planetary aspects this month could ruin your efforts. Chances of getting confused with your ideas will be abundant, so don't make any decisions or open your mouth without thinking.

The way you earn money will change. You have the opportunity for a major accomplishment in your work.

You need to be more tolerant with your partner, you can't be all the time thinking that the mistakes he/she makes are a reason to end the relationship.

Unfortunately, the consequences of decisions made months ago will affect you. You should put aside your ambitions and focus your attention on family matters. If you are planning changes in your professional area, it is better to wait until next year.

If you desire a relationship, love is waiting for you, there is an opportunity for a passionate romance on the horizon. At the end of the month with the holidays you may suffer from stomach problems, which should not be underestimated. Overweight people should start planning to lose weight in January. As you close out the year, things get out of hand or slow down.

Lucky numbers

5 - 11 - 16 - 34 - 36

The Tarot Cards, an Enigmatic and Psychological World.

The word Tarot means "royal road", it is a millenary practice, it is not known exactly who invented card games in general, nor the Tarot in particular; there are the most dissimilar hypotheses in this sense.

Some say that it arose in Atlantis or Egypt, but others believe that tarots came from China or India, from the ancient land of the gypsies, or that they arrived in Europe through the Cathars. The fact is that tarot cards distill astrological, alchemical, esoteric, and religious symbolism, both Christian and pagan.

Until recently, if you mentioned the word 'tarot' to some people, it was common for them to imagine a gypsy sitting in front of a crystal ball in a room surrounded by mysticism, or to think of black magic or witchcraft, but nowadays this has changed.

This ancient technique has been adapting to the new times, it has joined technology and many young people feel a deep interest in it.

Young people have isolated themselves from religion because they believe that they will not find the solution to what they need there, they realized the duality of this, something that does not happen with spirituality. All over the social networks you find accounts dedicated to the study and tarot readings, since everything related to esotericism is fashionable, in fact, some hierarchical decisions are made considering the tarot or astrology.

What is remarkable is that the predictions that are usually related to tarot are not the most sought after, the ones related to self-knowledge and spiritual counseling are the most requested.

The tarot is an oracle, through its drawings and colors, we stimulate our psychic sphere, the innermost part that goes beyond the natural. Many people turn to the tarot as a spiritual or psychological guide because we live in uncertain times, and this pushes us to seek answers in spirituality.

It is such a powerful tool that tells you concretely what is going on in your subconscious so that you can perceive it through the lens of a new wisdom.

Carl Gustav Jung, the famed psychologist, used the symbols of tarot cards in his psychological studies.

He created the theory of archetypes, where he discovered an extensive sum of images that help in analytical psychology.

The use of drawings and symbols to appeal to a deeper understanding is frequently used in psychoanalysis. These allegories are part of us, corresponding to symbols of our subconscious and our mind.

Our unconscious has dark areas, and when we use visual techniques, we can reach different parts of it and reveal elements of our personality that we do not know. When you can decode these messages through the pictorial language of tarot, you can choose what decisions to make in life to create the destiny you really want.

The tarot with its symbols teaches us that a different universe exists, especially nowadays where everything is so chaotic, and a logical explanation is sought for everything.

The World, Tarot Card for Leo 2024

Symbol of success, victory, and a comfortable life. It means the realization of your plans. It is the end and the beginning of something better, a new cycle in your life.

Your efforts will finally bear fruit, and it indicates that you have reached the end of a journey or have completed an important period in your life.

You have suffered hardships and challenges along the way, but these have only made you stronger and wiser. More experienced than when you first began the journey.

This Tarot card is an indicator of an important and inexorable change, of tectonic amplitude. This change represents an opportunity for you to put an end to the old and give a good start to the new.

It indicates maturity, a sense of inner balance and deeper understanding.

It suggests that you may be approaching a more mature understanding of your identity and the self-confidence that comes with age.

It also represents the fall of barriers, sometimes in a spiritual sense, but sometimes in a purely physical sense, indicating a future with travel.

Runes of the Year 2024

Runes are a set of symbols that form an alphabet. "Rune" means secret and symbolizes the noise of one stone colliding with another. Runes are an ancient visionary and magical method.

Runes do not serve for exact predictions, but they do serve to guide you about a future event, a subject, or a decision.

The runes have a specific meaning for the person who wants it, but also some message related to the adversities that arise in life.

Othila, Rune of Leo 2024

In ancient times, the Vikings gave extreme importance to the Othila rune as it symbolizes family welfare and the home.

Othila is a beneficial rune for acquiring property and investing in material things. It foretells success in what you start, personal development, and fulfilled goals. It predicts that you receive the reward for your courage and opportunities to advance arise.

This rune indicates that you should seek advice from professional people so that you can face the challenges ahead.

It is not easy to separate from those you love, but it is necessary to achieve your goals, which will also harm your family, social and work spheres. Take on the challenge and focus on the path you are starting on.

You must not have a three-dimensional life, it consumes you. You must be adaptable and skillful to change your course. You can't always run away, it's time to take the plunge, go the extra mile, and stand on your own two feet.

In health matters, he advises you to take a break and take a good rest. You have been very busy with many things at the same time, or you have simply been very active, this is why he recommends you stop.

Take a well-deserved vacation and recharge your energy, to come back with the best spirit and continue with your projects or start new things.

Lucky Colors

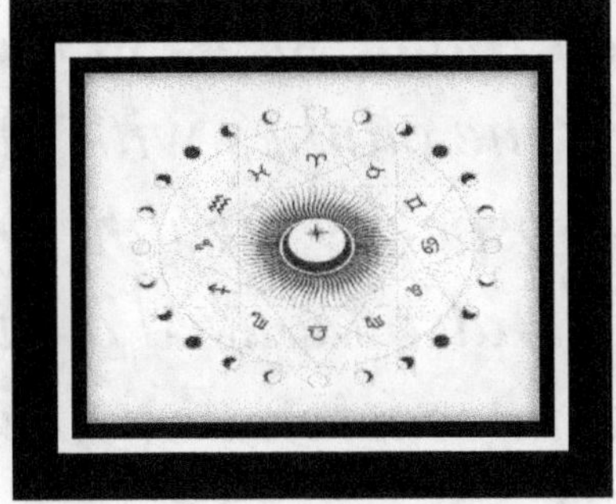

Colors affect us psychologically; they influence our appreciation of things, opinion about something or someone, and can be used to influence our decisions.

Traditions to welcome the new year vary from country to country, and on the night of December 31 we take stock of all the positive and negative things we experienced in the year that is leaving. We start thinking about what to do to transform our luck in the new year ahead.

There are several ways to attract positive energies towards us when we receive the new year, and one of them is to wear or wear accessories of a specific color that attracts what we wish for the year that is about to begin.

Colors have energetic charges that influence our lives, so it is always advisable to receive the year dressed in a color that attracts the energies of what we want to achieve.

For that there are colors that vibrate positively with each zodiac sign, so the recommendation is that you wear the clothes with the hue that will make you attract prosperity, health, and love in 2024. (These colors can also be used during the rest of the year for important occasions, or to enhance your days).

Remember that, although the most common is to wear red underwear for passion, pink for love and yellow or gold for abundance, it is never too much to include in our attire the color that most benefits our zodiac sign.

Lucky Color for Leo

Leo

Rosa

The key words of pink are *innocence, love, total surrender, and helping others.*

Pink is an emotionally relaxing color and influences feelings by making them gentle, soft, and deep.

It makes us feel affection, love, and protection. It also takes us away from loneliness and makes us sensitive people.

Just as red reflects more the sexual side, pink is associated with altruistic and true love.

Pink is the color of universal love, love for oneself and others, friendship, affection, harmony, inner peace.

Use pink when you want to encourage a relationship, be it friendship or romantic.

Lucky Charms

Who doesn't own a lucky ring, a chain that never comes off, or an object that they wouldn't give away for anything in the world? We all attribute a special power to certain items that belong to us and that special character that they assume for us makes them magical objects.

For a talisman to act and influence circumstances, its bearer must have faith in it, and this will transform it into a prodigious object, able to accomplish everything that is asked of it.

Usually, an amulet is any object that propitiates good as a preventive measure against evil, harm, disease, and witchcraft.

Amulets for good luck can help you to have a year 2024 full of blessings in your home, work, with your family, attract money and health. For the amulets to work properly you should not lend them to anyone else, and you should always have them at hand.

Amulets have existed in all cultures and are made from elements of nature that serve as catalysts of energies that help create human desires.

The amulet is assigned the power to ward off evils, spells, diseases, disasters or to counteract evil wishes cast through the eyes of others.

Amulet for Leo

Unicorn.

The unicorn symbolizes the hope for healing and the strength we all seek. The Unicorn can be used to amplify your psychic gifts.

The unicorn represents purity, unconditional love, and magic. This mythological creature has been revered for its divine strength and for being a source of energy that allows us to connect with the spiritual realm. The presence of the unicorn in your life will remind you that magic and love are always present, and that you are strong. It is an animal that attracts good luck and justice. As a symbol of purity and will protect and guard you from all evil.

Lucky Quartz

We are all attracted to diamonds, rubies, emeralds and sapphires, obviously precious stones. Semi-precious stones such as carnelian, tiger's eye, white quartz, and lapis lazuli are also highly prized as they have been used as ornaments and symbols of power for thousands of years.

What many do not know is that they were valued for more than their beauty: each had a sacred significance, and their healing properties were as important as their ornamental value.

Crystals still have the same properties in our days, most people are familiar with the most popular ones such as amethyst, malachite and obsidian, but nowadays there are new crystals such as larimar, petalite and phenacite that have become known.

A crystal is a solid body with a geometrically regular shape, crystals were formed when the earth was created and have continued to metamorphose as the planet has changed, crystals are the DNA of the earth, they are miniature stores that contain the development of our planet over millions of years.

Some have been bent to extraordinary pressures and others grew in chambers buried deep underground, others dripped into being. Whatever *form they take, their crystalline structure can absorb, conserve, focus and emit energy.*

At the heart of the crystal is the atom, its electrons, and protons. The atom is dynamic and is composed of a series of particles that rotate around the center in constant motion, so that, although the crystal may seem motionless, it is a living molecular mass that vibrates at a certain frequency, and this is what gives energy to the crystal.

Gems used to be a royal and priestly prerogative, the priests of Judaism wore a plaque on their chest full of precious stones which was much more than an emblem to designate their function, as it transferred power to the wearer.

Men have worn stones since the stone age as they had a protective function guarding their wearers from various evils. Today's crystals have the same power, and we can select our jewelry not only according to their external attractiveness, having them near us can boost our energy (orange carnelian), clean the space around us (amber) or attract wealth (citrine).

Certain crystals such as smoky quartz and black tourmaline can absorb negativity, emitting a pure and clean energy.

Wearing a black tourmaline around the neck protects from electromagnetic emanations including that of cell phones, a citrine will not only attract wealth, but will also help you keep it, place it in the wealthy part of your home (the back left most away from the front door).

If you are looking for love, crystals can help you, place a rose quartz in the relationship corner of your house (the back right corner furthest away from the front door) its effect is so powerful that you may want to add an amethyst to offset the attraction.

You can also use rhodochrosite, love will come your way.

Crystals can heal and give balance, some crystals contain minerals known for their therapeutic properties, malachite has a high concentration of copper, wearing a malachite bracelet allows the body to absorb minimal amounts of copper.

Lapis lazuli relieves migraine, but if the headache is caused by stress, amethyst, amber or turquoise placed above the eyebrows will relieve it.

Quartz and minerals are jewels of mother earth, give yourself the opportunity, and connect with the magic they give off.

Lucky Quartz for Leo 2024

Carnelian

Positive quartz for those who have trouble concentrating, who are mentally alienated or complicated in life. It gives courage and protection. It is indicated for melancholic people.

It is used as a talisman in homes and businesses as a defense against the evil eye, and envy. It is connected to the energy of authority and passion.

It is recommended for professional success, to reassure doubts and to give mental clarity when a professional decision must be made.

For those who find it difficult to speak in public, carnelian helps them to have the courage to face this obstacle. It is suggested for those who have nervous problems, since the energetic projection of the quartz helps to achieve sleep and be calm, therefore, it favors physical and mental rest.

Leo and Vocation

Leo has an excellent sense of integrity. He is faithful, and with many personal values. He always tries to make decisions according to what he believes is right, without harming the needs or interests of others.

He has a noble heart and values loyalty above all else. They cannot stand betrayal, sneaky behavior, or lack of values. This makes them very likable, and their positive attitude and hard work push them to different vocations and to excel in whatever they do.

Best Professions

Their ability to assume leadership roles makes them good bosses, and this always puts them in the spotlight or in positions of power. They are very sociable and good-natured. Positions of authority, acting, politics, high risk sports and presidents.

Compatibility of Leo and the Zodiac Signs

Symbolized by the lion, this sign will not let you forget him. Although his character is cheerful, he also has a fierce harshness that accompanies his howl. Everything Leo does is tragic and when he gets angry, it is best to stay out of his way. It is a fixed sign, very firm in its ideas, constant in its purposes and obstinate in its way of acting.

Leo is a diligent accomplice who puts his heart into every relationship. Of course, he can also be incredibly intransigent, but stubbornness is always a flash of his honesty.
Leo is inspired by drama, but also deeply sensitive, Leo is undoubtedly the most emotional of all the fire signs and is easily hurt so your partner will need to know how to nurture this tender specimen.

Loyalty is very important to Leo, so when you enter his domain, he will ask for absolute love. When this sign feels hurt, it is best not to give him advice, Leo seeks relief, not reminders, and so he will feel betrayed by his partner if you start giving your opinion on any situation.

Leo will take you to the edge because he loves to be challenged, since childhood he knows he is zodiacal royalty and even the most prudent lion will have a regal posture.

This sign never tires of receiving applause. Opulent dinners, exclusive parties and designer clothes make him feel loved. When looking for him, keep in mind that it's not easy to follow his rhyme. At times it can be difficult to date such a rigorous sign. But it's worth it in the end.

Once you reserve your place in Leo's heart, you will not want to give up the throne. Leo doesn't mind if his partner has an ego, on the contrary, the lion wants his partner to be vain and very self-confident. Leo is not looking for an egomaniac, but this fearless creature must make sure that his partner knows how to wear the crown with dignity.

Leo values the concept of a partner as an extension of himself. Since this fire sign is known for its boldness in everything from its creative ventures to its Hollywood-style romances, it's important to match with someone who knows verbatim what they're looking for.

When it comes to sexuality, the fiery Leo can also shine in bed. The lion's greatest sexual arousal is to feel desired. He is bewitched by seduction, and affection must be displayed through ostentatious trysts and grandiose romantic expressions. This sign howls at the thought of being coveted, especially when that burning desire translates into passionate love.
This fiery lion is always falling in love, likes his romances to be as big as his personality, and nothing makes him howl louder than unabashed adoration. He

needs to be the center of attention, and so he may be seduced by dangerous romances.

Leo doesn't find it easy to resist praise, so he gravitates towards compliments. If the drama ends prematurely and Leo is abandoned, it is another story. At first, his reaction is usually one of shock and after this phase, he experiences devastating anxiety showing his suffering.

Even if things get serious, the lion is an invulnerable creature who will find his way back to the light because Leo is cheerful and fearless, refusing to accept failure. Leo is always looking for a partner who will stimulate his spirit because in the end he hates boredom.

***Leo and Aries**, it is a relationship of pure fire where it is not easy to contain the flames. These signs nurture each other, creating an enthusiastic partnership based on desire and daring. Aries gladly understands Leo's dominating charisma. Aries, who also needs a lot of affection, is comforted by the nobility and warmth of his comrade the lion. Although both signs are self-confident, their generosity manifests itself very unevenly. Leo always carries his heart in his hand, while Aries' main concern is to emerge triumphant. Although these signs can give their best in a relationship, they also need to keep their egos in* *check. Otherwise, the relationship between Leo and Aries may eventually die out.*

Leo and Taurus *are loyal and dutiful individuals, but their pedantry and stubbornness can sometimes lead to major oppositions. Taurus dislikes Leo's magnificence, and the lion finds himself grumbling at the bull's obstinacy.*

As a couple, Leo and Taurus should check that their motives are not overly materialistic but adopt a more indifferent attitude that endorses an equal partnership. After all, Leo and Taurus have a lot in common, they both like the good things in life. So, if the two of them focus on their similarities, rather than their differences, they will enjoy an entertaining relationship.

Leo and Gemini *are a relationship that is initially sexy and daring. Leo needs to feel like a king, and somehow, Gemini always has connections to the most important places in town. However, at the end of the day, Leo wants to wrap up warm with a loyal partner. Unfortunately, Gemini may not be able to exercise that role as he wishes to continue to party. In this relationship both must learn to adjust to the needs of the other. Leo must rely on Gemini's perpetual cordiality, and Gemini must revere Leo's emotional* *fidelity. When these two signs are on the same page, this couple is efficient, frolicsome and a lot of fun.*

Leo and Cancer, *not a comfortable relationship. Leo is overwhelmed by Cancer's moodiness, and Cancer resents Leo's excessive dramatics. If these two are determined to make their relationship work, they will have to unite around their shared values such as loyalty, family, and honesty. Leo and Cancer are also likely to lift each other up, helping each other reach their full potential through friendship. For there to be no conflict, this couple must come to an agreement, and respect the terms.*

Leo and Leo, it's the most majestic couple in the zodiac. Leo loves to celebrate their luminosity, so when two lions get together, they spend most of their relationship talking about their love. This combination is a precipitous one that's bound to be filled with smiles, nobility, and plenty of idolatry. But no reign is perfect, and since Leo has a rather exaggerated ego, expect opposition. Whether they're fighting for the spotlight, the phone, or flattery, their mutual need for praise can put pressure on the relationship. However, the lion can calm down, so for this relationship to work each must often stroke the other's hair and reserve time for passion.*

Leo and Virgo, *although an unlikely pairing in principle, the fiery Leo and the idealistic Virgo can draw positive qualities from each other. Each sign should be aware that this relationship will require a great deal of understanding, tolerance and, perhaps most importantly, integrity and loyalty. At first, Virgo admires Leo's eccentricity and social subtlety. Leo takes satisfaction in this idolatry, until the luster begins to dissipate. Virgo has a habit of idealizing, but since nothing is perfect, this earth sign can quickly become disillusioned. For this pairing to work, it is important for each sign to make sure that the relationship is established for the right reason, making sure that the relationship is not ego driven.*

Leo and Libra *are an efficient relationship, when together, the generous Leo and the exquisite Libra bring their best attributes to the relationship. Together, they are enormously sociable and incomparably fun, attributes that are stabilized by Libra's gift. However, because Libra likes to keep the peace, he tends to be rather hesitant. Leo demands courageous loyalty, so Libra's preoccupation can be frustrating. Libra may feel a bit smothered by Leo's possessiveness. However, if they can reconcile their differences, Leo and Libra will feel great.*

Leo and Scorpio, *although the energy of fire can sometimes feel limited by water, this relationship is a* *powerful combination. Both are fixed signs, have strong beliefs and firm views. As a result, there is an obvious tension between these two signs, which can lead to some arguments and, perhaps most importantly some first-class sex. Leo is especially seduced by Scorpio's mysterious nature, while Scorpio is stimulated by Leo. However, these two must give themselves time to establish intimacy. Since Leo and Scorpio have such different ways of gliding through the world, each needs to learn to perceive the nuance of the other. Once trust is established, neither Leo nor Scorpio will want to separate.*

***Leo and Sagittarius**, it is an effective relationship. Leo has a fiery flame, but contained, it only needs an audience. Sagittarius, on the other hand, knows no limits. Consequently, Leo tends to lean towards this sign that admires him. Sagittarius also appreciates Leo's brilliance, although in this relationship he always tries to be free. A Leo-Sagittarius couple can spend hours talking, laughing, and bewitching each other with dynamic stories and witty banter.*

***Leo and Capricorn** are different creatures, Capricorn's seriousness is focused on long-term benefits, while Leo is driven by fame and fortune. Magically, however, Leo and Capricorn make an excellent romantic couple. Both signs are very insatiable, so although their techniques are different,* *they revere each other, and any arguments that arise will be circumstantial.*

When they work together, Leo and Capricorn can achieve greatness. Capricorn teaches Leo the capacity for abstraction, and Leo teaches Capricorn the art of having a good time. If they invest fully in their relationship, they will reap great rewards.

Leo and Aquarius, *being opposite signs, are an interesting couple. While Leo symbolizes the ruler, Aquarius represents humanity. When coupled together, they can create a system of checks and balances for each other, driven by justice and progressive thinking. This relationship exists in a beautiful and abundant realm, yet occasionally Aquarius sees Leo as selfish.*

In this relationship, both must strive to understand the other's perspective. To do so successfully, Leo must restrain their ego and Aquarius must elevate their compassion. This relationship has incredible potential, so healthy compromise will surely be rewarded.

Leo and Pisces, it *is an excellent relationship. Leo is happiest when it can freely emit its radiant, tropical light. Pisces is interconnected with the sea, and just as the ocean reflects the Sun's light in the distance, Pisces is happy to welcome, and even enhance, Leo's vibrant luminosity. While this relationship can be* *effective and seductive, it is important that the majestic lion not be engulfed by the extreme sensitivity of Pisces.*

To ensure a happy relationship, both of you must be committed to embracing each other's strongest qualities, applauding your differences with kind appreciation and genuine respect.

Signs not to do business with

Taurus, Gemini and Scorpio, the connections between these signs are weak to differences.

Signs to be associated with

Capricorn, Libra, and Pisces. They are signs that have practical sense and know how to invest money. They are responsible and serious. They know how to invest in business.

Money Rituals

Spell to Get a Job.

You need:

- 1 white candle

- 1 combined yellow and black candle

- 1 red cloth bag

- 1 yellow ribbon

- 2 sheets of yellow paper

- Bee jelly

- Ruda

- Coal

- 1 citrine quartz

- 1 perfume or lavender

- New sewing needle

- New large glass dish

You write on the white candle your full name, to write it you use the new needle, which you will later bury in the yard of your house. Light the white candle.

Then on one of the sheets of yellow paper you write the request to get the new job, include specific details such as the money you want to earn and the position you want; spread the bee jelly on it, fold it into four parts and place it on the new plate.

Mentalize your request and repeat it during the whole ritual. Next to the plate place the bag with the rue that you will use for the incense, a few drops of perfume and the citrine quartz.

Next, you light the charcoal and add the rue on top of it. You will start the incense from the farthest point from the entrance door, that is, from the back to the front; then you let it extinguish by itself, near the ritual.

On the other yellow paper, you write the full name of the person. With this paper you wrap the bicolor candle, light it, and place it near the plate, the bag used as a talisman and the bottle of perfume (always open), then repeat three times: "Here and now all my wishes are fulfilled for my personal progress and that of my family". Place the citrine inside the bag and close it with the yellow ribbon. When the candle burns out, the bag serves as an amulet.

Spell to Get a Better Job.

You need:

- 1 combined yellow and red candle.

- 1 red candle

- 1 black candle

- 7 yellow candles

- 1 paper cartridge

- Honey

- Coal.

- Eucalyptus incense

- 3 leaves of rue

- 3 mint leaves

- 1 bottle of perfume

- 1 new metal tray

- 1 new sewing needle

You write on the bicolor candle with the needle your full name. On the black candle, the name of the company.

In the green one, the job you aspire to and in the red candle, again your full name.

On the cartridge paper you must specify the job you wish to obtain or the business you work for.

This paper must be spread with honey, folded in four parts, and placed on the tray.

On the seven yellow candles you write with the needle the job you want.

When you have everything ready, light the charcoal and place the rue and mint leaves on it, with a few drops of the chosen perfume.

Leave it burning while you light the bicolor candle and place it near the candle with the paper (the one you spread with honey).

Light all the following candles with the same flame: the black candle, which you will place on the left side of the tray, the green candle on the right side and the red candle in the center.

The leftovers can be thrown away in the trash.

Spell for Success in Job Interviews.

Place in a green bag three leaves of sage, basil, parsley, and rue. Add a tiger eye quartz and a malachite. Close the bag with a golden ribbon. To activate it you put it in your left hand at the level of your heart and then a few centimeters above you put *your right hand, close your eyes, and imagine a white energy coming from your right hand to your left hand covering the bag. Keep it in your purse or pocket.*

Cleaning to Get Customers.

Crush ten shelled hazelnuts and a sprig of parsley in a mortar and pestle. Boil two liters of Full Moon water and add the crushed ingredients. Let them boil for 10 minutes and then strain it. With this infusion you will clean the floor of your business, from the entrance door to the bottom of it. You must repeat this cleaning every Monday and Thursday for a month, if possible, at the time of the planet Mercury.

Spell to Create an Economic Shield for your Business.

You need:

- 5 yellow flower petals

- Sunflower seeds

- Sun-dried lemon peel

- Wheat flour

- 3 coins of common use

Crush the yellow flowers and sunflower seeds in a mortar and pestle, then add the lemon peel and the wheat flour.

Mix the ingredients well and store them together with the three coins in a hermetically sealed jar.

You should use this preparation every morning before leaving your house. You should introduce in the bottle the fingertips of the five fingers of the left hand first and then of the right hand, then rub it on the palms of your hands.

Ritual to Avoid Losing Your Job.

You need:

- 1 large rusty nail

- 1 small cup of guava candy

- 1 small plastic bag

- 1 yellow cloth sachet

- 1 orange candle

- 1 violet candle

- 3 bay leaves

- 1 needle and thread

 Place the orange and violet candle on the edge of a window, between them place the cup of guava candy. Light the candles. Insert the nail into the candy so that it is not visible. While you do it repeat in your mind: "I am a person who deserves this job, spiritual guides protect my work, my money and my energies". The next day you take out the clove and without cleaning it, put it inside the plastic bag and then inside the yellow bag together with the three bay leaves. You should place this bag in the place where you work.

Ritual to Make an Excellent Impression on the First Day of Work.

You need:

- 2 nails of 5 cm (new)

- 1 piece of purple ribbon

- 1 piece of white ribbon

- 1 purple candle

- 1 white candle

It is most effective if you do it on a Wednesday at the time of planet Mercury.

You must write with one of the nails the name of the business where you are going to work on the purple candle, then leave it next to it. Then you write your name on the white candle with the other nail. Take the nail with which you wrote on the purple candle and bury it in the middle of the candle, while you do this repeat in your mind "As this nail reaches the heart of the candle, my aura will envelop my bosses and work colleagues" (heat the nail first to facilitate this operation). Immediately put the other nail in the white candle and repeat in your mind "My guardian angel protects me and guides me to success". Light the candles and when they are spent, pick up the two nails and tie them with the ribbons.

You should keep them in your office.

Magic Recipe to Increase Fortune

You need:

- 1 rose of Jericho

- Flowery water

- Lavender green

- Citrine quartz

- Tiger eye quartz

- Full Moon Water

Place the essences in a glass container with the Full Moon water.

Then you place the quartz and the rose of Jericho. You should place this container as an ornament in your business or office.

Spell for Abundance in your Work.

You need:

- 7 earthenware vessels

- Virgin bee honey

- Mint leaves

Mix the honey and mint leaves, distribute the contents in clay containers and distribute them in your home or work office.

You must perform this spell on the first day of the month at the time of the planet Jupiter.

To strengthen this ritual when you are distributing the containers repeat out loud: "I sweeten my life, my home and office and I invoke the four elements to bring me success and money, here and now in perfect harmony and for the good of all".

Best Countries and Cities to Live In

Countries: France, Italy, Republic of Macedonia, United States and Romania.

Cities: Bohemia, Sicily, Rome, Ravenna, Bath, Bristol, Taunton, Prague, Damascus, Basra, Apulia, Philadelphia, Los Angeles, Chicago, and Bombay.

Incenses and Essential Oils for Money

Incense and Lemon Essential Oil: possesses mystical properties, relieves stress, and attracts joy.

Plants for Money

Mint: mint has always been known for its medicinal properties, but the simple fact of having it at home helps to eliminate bad vibrations and attract economic prosperity.

Quartz for Money

Turquoise: *It is a quartz that attracts luck and money. The energies of protection and abundance that it emanates protect economic stability. as personal.*

Money Charms

The Pentacles of Jupiter that will guarantee you Prosperity.

Pentacles are magical figures, capable of transmitting positive energies to their environment. The action of Jupiter's pentacles derives from the combination of letters, signs, and beneficial formulas, they symbolize graphically and mystically a wish. They clearly act on the psyche of people who have visual contact with him.

The largest compilation of pentacles is found in The Clavicles of King Solomon, a volume of high magic attributed to this biblical king. In it are 36 pentacles that have various purposes and among them are the seven pentacles of Jupiter.

Pentacles To Prosper.

The purpose of these pentacles is to provide abundance, to resolve work-related conflicts and to help you perceive more directly all kinds of benefits that grant greater prosperity.

Jupiter, the so-called Great Benefic in astrology, is a planet that is related to expansion, optimism, links with powerful people and the ability to make fortune. You should draw them with great concentration and with the intention that they manifest your will. The most suitable material is a piece of parchment. Once finished, they should be hung somewhere visible, such as the cash register or in your wallet (you can print them).

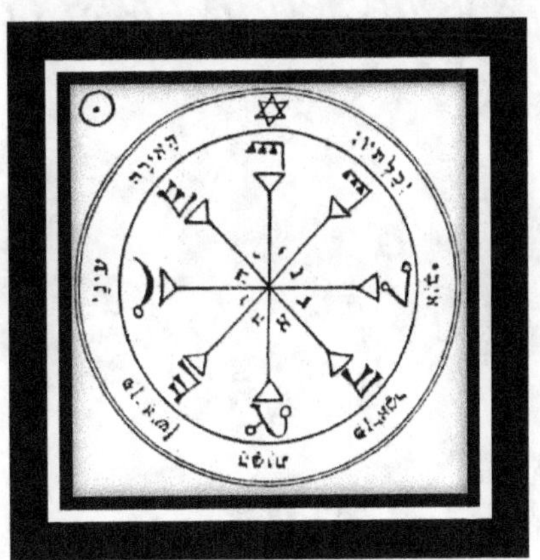

Affirmations to Receive Money

You should perform these decrees for 21 days so that you can see the results, if possible three times a day. If you repeat them out loud, they will be more powerful.

I am infinite love, the source of wealth, abundance, prosperity.

I am perfect abundance and divine wealth.

I am prosperity in my business and finances.

I am the divine wisdom that intelligently shapes all existence. I walk safely through abundance. I see myself in prosperity.

Vacations

Vacations provide physical and mental benefits. It has been proven that vacationing lowers stress levels and benefits the immune system. Sometimes planning a vacation causes stress because there are infinite options and deciding becomes a chimerical task.

Using astrology, understanding your personality provides insight into the ideal vacation spot for you.

Aries, *an all-inclusive resort with outdoor sports activities in a warm location such as Punta Cana, Cancun and the Turks and Caicos Islands would be ideal. Australia is an exciting country that offers a wealth of emotions to make your heart race.*

Taurus, *a stay in a luxurious resort on Cayman Island, or a luxurious vacation in Dubai, in a hotel that has all the amenities will be very appealing. Italy is a perfect country because there you will find everything you have always dreamed of love, charm, luxury, wonderful food, and first-class wines.*

Gemini *loves to feel intellectually engaged. Travel with guided excursions such as a safari in Africa or researching the species of the Galapagos Islands offer the zodiac communicator a luxurious experience.*

Cancer, *short trips, surrounded by family and friends. Disney World, enjoying the attractions and its diverse foods is one option. In Orlando, Florida, there are multiple fantastic hotels and resorts, each with a unique and fascinating theme.*

Leo, *staying in a bungalow over the sea in Tahiti is fantastic for this sign. Another luxury alternative, something the lion loves, would be to rent a private tropical island in the Maldives, Fiji, or the Virgin Islands.*

Virgo, *Italy is your best option. This country will keep you well occupied. As an earth sign you connect with the world around you, places like La Romana in the Dominican Republic, Puerto Viejo in Costa Rica, and Belo Horizonte in Brazil will inject life into you.*

Libra, *go for cities with museums. Tropical vacations will not be as satisfying for Libra as touring the Louvre in Paris, the Acropolis Museum in Athens, Greece, the Prado Museum in Madrid, Spain or the Uffizi Gallery in Florence, Italy.*

Scorpion, *spend a few days on a secluded beach with liquor and massages. In Greece, Bali, St. Martin, or Hawaii you will find all these luxuries. Visiting heritage sites near your luxury hotel would be an extraordinary combination of tropical and cultural vacation. Mykonos and Roda in Greece are perfect destinations.*

Sagittarius, *explore the Camino de Santiago, a network of very different paths, all leading to the city of Santiago de Compostela. Each path has its history, heritage, and magic. Sagittarius is a traveler who craves new experiences so in Ireland you will find everything you are looking for.*

Capricorn, *a goal-oriented sign. Vacations where you can make new business relationships. China would be spectacular. Capricorn has a sense of historical value that other signs do not have, so countries like Israel and Egypt where history is present will make you feel at home.*

Aquarius *loves new ideas, unknown places, and new relationships. A fantastic country to visit would be Japan not only for its fascinating history and culture,* *but because each of its regions has something different to offer.*

__Pisces__, a water sign that is happy with tropical vacations. A beachfront hotel would be ideal. The island "La Dique" in the Republic of Seychelles, perhaps the most beautiful beach in the world will be a sure success. Pisces, possessing a calm outlook on life, being ruled by Neptune makes you a creative thinker. Sweden is a country he should visit because there he will find a culture as innovative as he is.

Who is your soul mate according to your zodiac sign?

When we hear the term "soul mates," we usually think of them as referring to members of a couple, i.e., someone with whom you have a strong sentimental-sexual connection. However, legitimate soul mates do not always relate to each other from that point of view, and often are not even interested in the sexual aspect of a relationship.

Your soul mate may not only be your partner, but also your parent, friend, child, grandparent, boss, or sister.

From an astrological point of view and considering that the lessons we need to learn before reaching the next spiritual level are the ones that define the type of affective relationships, we need to develop in life today, we can say that Cancer and Pisces are soul mates of Aries.

With Cancer and Pisces, Aries can not only focus better and resolve conflicts without violence, but also develop empathy, that is, the ability to put themselves in the other's place and learn to share.

These two signs do not like conflicts, and if they do arise, they prefer dialogue to any episode of brutality.

Aries can teach Cancer and Pisces not to need the approval of others, to be more risk-taking, and not to try to please everyone, i.e., to be more assertive.

The sensual Taurus, enemy of change, inbred relative of inertia, has as his soul mate Sagittarius and Gemini, two signs that know that life is a fascinating journey, but not a static one.

They can teach Taurus that it does not have to stay where it no longer must be for fear of uncertainty, and that there will always be certain situations or circumstances that will happen without us expecting them, and without us possessing any power to modify them. Taurus also has a lot to teach these signs.

Lessons of willpower, to have commitments with others, to be committed to what they do and to continue to the end with persistence, without haste or slowness. To have principles, and to be prudent.

Leo can balance a lot of karma with their soul mates belonging to Libra and Aquarius.

A Leo may become obstinate with a wrong idea or belief out of vanity; Libra and Aquarius know that behind an egocentric person there is a low self-esteem.

Libra will teach Leo equanimity and tolerance, to use reasoning and diplomacy to maintain smooth communication. Aquarius, the opposite sign to Leo, equipped with objective and fair judgment as they are never swayed by prejudice, will teach Leo to see people's hearts, to offer their shoulder and give sympathetic words in times of need.

Leo never hesitates when making decisions, and if they do, they do not manifest it, something that Libra should practice.

Fidelity is a hallmark in Leo, something unknown to Aquarius, and the little lions can give him moral lessons.

Virgo, known as perfectionists because of their immense fear of failure, has Scorpio and Capricorn as soul mates. Virgo likes to be rigorous in their decisions and has a prototype in almost every aspect of their life. This selectivity holds them back from following the movement of life.

Virgo will literally tear an entire project apart if they feel it wasn't perfect in the first place, something a Capricorn would never do as their vision will allow them to see that alternative measures can always be taken, without having to start over.

Capricorn is a sign sure of their own space, they don't make meaningless decisions, something Virgo sometimes does.

On the other hand, Scorpio can mitigate the worst and enhance the best of Virgo. Scorpio and Virgo have a practical approach to life; however, Scorpio is much more of a life-lover than Virgo. Scorpio will bring the decisiveness that Virgo lacks, and Virgo will bring control and rationality to the passionate Scorpio.

Virgo will make Capricorn more pleasant and playful at his side, isolating him from that excessive seriousness that he often shows in his face.

The madness

Madness has been revealed throughout history as an obscure, enigmatic, and conflicting truth. It has frightened us, we have ignored it and even accepted it, and as a result, the people who have supposedly suffered from it have been rejected, eliminated, and honored.

Any behavior that is incongruent with our reasoning is not necessarily an act of insanity, but a different way of proceeding.

It is a mistake if, when we feel affected or annoyed by the actions or follies of others, we banish them, since this does not make us more reasonable, balanced, or perfect, but rather makes us just as crazy.

Defining insanity is as complex as defining sanity, but all zodiac signs have their degree of insanity.

Cancer: They are temperamental. This causes them to have an incomprehensible personality seen from the outside. The popularity of crazy people was earned by their inconsistent character that sometimes disturbs the people around them.

Scorpio: They need change to be happy, they can do crazy things just to generate some action. For them having an outburst is normal because they are addicted to change and frenzies.

Pisces: *It is impossible for them not to infect you with their madness. Their instability and imbalance bother the people around them. They see everything as rosy, which makes them be called crazy because they are always floating on a cloud.*

Gemini: *He is famous for his duality. They are sometimes in conflict with themselves. They love challenges that involve danger. They love to plan impromptu adventures and are always ready to border the limits of maximum madness.*

Leo: *When the fire settles in their head, they think that everything that surrounds their life is more urgent than anything else. They are extravagant and have attitudes that for others are considered crazy. They can do things that a reasonable person would never do.*

Aries: *They upset themselves and anyone around them. They are stubborn and like to be the first in everything, even if for that they must commit crazy* *things. They do not know how to take it back, something that leads them to perform irrational acts.*

Aquarius: *A rebellious and free sign, which does not care in the least about the opinion they have of them. It acts in a capricious way, with crazy attitudes that break the paradigms.*

Sagittarius: *He is fun, but violent with his desire for action. They do not know how to measure the consequences of their actions, something that many consider madness. It is not strange to see them totally unbridled, crossing the terrain of irresponsibility.*

Libra: *They long for happiness and harmony, and to get it they are willing to do anything crazy. They are unstable, and that leads them to break their commitments, something that many consider crazy.*

Virgo: *They go to extremes and become obsessive. They have a vision of what they want written in stone, no one can give them advice, they do not let themselves be guided. When they do not listen, they commit various follies.*

Taurus*: When an idea lands in their mind there is no one to banish it, even committing crazy things to corroborate their hypothesis. Try to test their patience and you will discover how far their level of madness goes.*

Capricorn*: He forgets absolutely nothing, does not forgive and much less, forgets, if you do something wrong, do not worry because he will remind you for a lifetime to drive you completely crazy. Capricorn is insanely obsessive about control.*

The psychology behind the lottery.

Lottery games are very popular all over the world.

We all have the impossible dream of winning the lottery, since the illusion of being millionaires, by a stroke of luck, even if the odds are minimal, is the main reason why people play.

Players perceive that the cost of the lottery ticket, in relation to the profits they would obtain if they won, is miniscule. We always perceive risk emotionally, and if it causes us pleasure, we tend to see the risk as insignificant and neutralize the emotion of danger, focusing only on the benefits.

Players see the lottery as a unique opportunity to be rewarded by investing little money, and with little exposure to risk.

Games have both traditional and superstitious aspects. Some people always play the same numbers because they are their favorites, relate them to a significant date, or have dreamed them.

Others play at a specific time, day, or place. When we think we are in control, we feel confident, because when we choose the numbers ourselves, instead of playing at random, although the chances of being right are the same, we have the impression that we are controlling destiny, and that the chances are in our favor.

There are people who only play for fun, in these cases the lottery transcends the economic cost, becoming a fun that is enlivened when they conjecture everything, they can do with the money they would acquire.

There are five psychological descriptions of individual lottery players:

The adventurer, *who is bewitched by games involving large sums of money, speculating with random numbers, and with planned numbers.*

The competitor, *who insists on showing off through gambling that he bets to win.*

The greedy, *who has no boundaries for gambling, and is not afraid to take risks when betting.*

The tactician, *never playing risky, looks for tactics, strategies, and numerical sets when playing the numbers.*

The superstitious person, *who always plays the same number combinations, uses talismans, rituals, or will buy his tickets on a specific date and place.*

Is there a trick or formula to win the lottery?

That question is still unanswered. There are many who speculate, and claim, that you are more likely to be struck by lightning before you win the lottery. Although others study the odds with great perseverance and subtlety.

Playing the lottery, or any other game of chance if it is done with measure, is a cheap way to buy illusions and confidence in the future. The complication arises when the person does not control his impulses to play, generating an addiction to gambling and falling into compulsive gambling.

A gambling addict is an individual to whom gambling causes great difficulties at work and in his family relationships, since losses induce him to gamble larger amounts of money with the aspiration of recovering the lost money. This becomes a vicious circle, and the only way to solve it is with psychotherapeutic treatment.

The best gifts for zodiac signs

Gift giving is a universal way to show that we care and appreciate a person, but gift buying can be a challenge, for some a real headache.

The planets can help you once, knowing the zodiac sign of the person, you may be able to make the ideal gift.

Fire signs: Aries, Leo and Sagittarius *like gifts that make them feel important, related to sports, travel, and technology.*

A professional digital camera, the latest model of iPhone, a plane ticket with hotel included to an exotic tourist spot or with historical background, business books, sportswear or exercise equipment, lottery tickets, bottles of fine wine and exclusive branded shoes will please these signs greatly.

Taurus, Virgo and Capricorn*, who belong to the earth element, are sometimes traditional, but that doesn't mean they don't like gifts from recognized brands.*

A painting of a famous painter, a belt or briefcase to carry their work papers, a wallet with their initials, branded perfumes, massages or body treatments, a pet, bathrobes, cozy pajamas, or even aromatherapy diffusers will make them happy.

Air signs: Gemini, Libra and Aquarius are not materialistic, and the functionality of a gift is much more important than the price. Their imagination is abundant, and anything that stimulates this capacity appeals to them.

A cell phone, computer or IPad, books on personal growth, spirituality, philosophy and alternative therapies, self-help and economic empowerment courses, a telescope, tickets to the opera or theater, an animal that does not have to be caged, quartz, essential oils, incense, and after-bath colognes will be highly appreciated by these signs.

Cancer, Scorpio and Pisces, the water signs, will love personalized gifts. Cooking utensils, a romantic dinner on the beach under the moonlight, a relaxing massage in a spa, daring lingerie, slippers or a comfortable sofa to watch TV, a bottle of champagne, scented candles, amulets, astrology books, a set of tarot cards, lotions, perfumes and beauty accessories, wine, cookies, preserves and all variety of gourmet products are on the list of gifts that these signs will accept with great pleasure.

Giving gifts is a blessing, it is a gesture of generosity; giving gifts is a symbolic act that represents a compliment, an attention to someone we want to please and symbolizes the affection we profess.

When we give gifts, relationships are improved and strengthened, and joy is generated.

The zodiac signs and their fears.

The twelve signs of the zodiac symbolize twelve essential archetypes of the human personality, but at the same time they are psychological prototypes, which is why each of the zodiac signs has a very specific and personal fear.

Let us remember that fear is an essential human alarm and defense mechanism. It only becomes a problem when it is excessive.

Fears are insecurities and sometimes we project them with the opposite actions as it is the case of the **Aries** sign; recognized for their iron will, nothing and nobody paralyzes them. They love to control everything, and their most ingrained fear is to fail or ask for help, because for them this is synonymous of weakness.

Taurus is the most stubborn of the earth signs. Change terrifies them, as well as running out of money, they spend their lives saving because poverty frightens them.

Gemini, the communicator of the zodiac, a bit anxious and insecure, they try to attract attention because they dread looking boring. Legitimate children of the

Moon, Cancers love their safety zone because no one can hurt them there, they are terrified of loneliness and rejection.

Leo, the king of the zodiac, leaders and brave, were not born to lose. Their most ingrained fear is to go unnoticed; they prefer to be spoken ill of, but not to be ignored.

The master of neatness **Virgo** sometimes becomes compulsive about health, so they are hypochondriacs. Their main fear is getting sick, but disorganization scares them more than anything else.

 Exceptionally intelligent **Librans** are indecisive and therein lies their primary fear: making decisions. Another of their fears is loneliness.

The enigmatic and seductive **Scorpios** have an elephant's memory, they fear betrayal and if you do something they dislike, they will keep it from you forever. Never keep a secret from a Scorpio.

The adventurer of the zodiac, **Sagittarius is** terrified of commitment because the demands are terrifying. They are very funny, but behind that smile hides the fear of being deceived.

Demanding to the extreme, **Capricorns** never stray from their goals; their main fear is to make mistakes, especially at the professional level. They are self-sacrificing and fear not achieving their dreams.

The rebellious and utopian **Aquarius** fear losing their freedom, this would mean losing their own essence. They always have many friendships, but none of them bind them. They need the group, but do not want the group to need them.

Peace is synonymous with **Pisces**, they hate confrontations. Compassionate to the core, they are afraid to see others suffer. They are a little insecure, have stage fright and fear rejection.

Some old astrology books hold Saturn totally responsible for fear in a natal chart, I think that for fear to originate, the alliance of several planets with their corresponding energies must manifest.

That is, fears are represented by various planets linked by aspects, there is no specific planet that is necessarily related to the development of any type of fear.

Moon in Leo

If your Moon is in Leo, you express your emotions with passion and intensity, you love to be the center of attention and give a dramatic touch to your feelings.

Ideally, you want to be appreciated, but with the Moon in Leo any attention is better than none. If you sense that you are being ignored, you will feel threatened, and when this happens, your instincts prompt you to pretend.

In other words, if you are the center of attention, you will be happy and feel safe.

In a perfect world everything would be focused on you, but since the world is not perfect, you are not the center of attention.

With the Moon in Leo your challenge is not to discover your security needs, but to make sure that the items on your priority list are appropriate.

You must analyze each relationship and determine when it is appropriate for you to be the center of attention. Be aware of your reactions.

Profile your inner self so that others will appreciate you for who you are.

People with the Moon in Leo are warm and generous with their family members, empathetic and loyal. They are prone to have a jealous emotional nature, although they are not possessive. They need a partner whom they can impress. These energies make them difficult to relate to emotionally.

Their feelings are hurt when they feel they are ignored.

They instinctively feel strong emotions, are dramatic and creative. The Moon in Leo is associated with children, so they enjoy play and fun. Spending time with children helps them expand their creativity and fun.

People with Moon in Leo have leadership qualities that inspire. They encourage people to commit to results, while at the same time enjoying the journey.

The importance of the Ascendant Sign

The Sun sign has a major impact on who we are, but the Ascendant is what really defines us, and that could even be the reason why you don't identify with some traits of your zodiac sign.

Really the energy that your sun sign gives you makes you feel different from the rest of the people, for that reason, when you read your horoscope sometimes you feel identified and gives sense to some predictions, and that happens because it helps you to understand how you could feel and what will happen to you, but it only shows you a percentage of what could really be.

The Ascendant is different from the Sun sign because it reflects who we are superficially, that is, how others see you or the energy you transmit to people, and this is so real that you may meet someone and if you predict their sign, you may have discovered their Ascendant sign and not their Sun sign.

In summary, the characteristics you see in someone when you first meet them is the Ascendant, but since our lives are affected by the way we relate to others, the Ascendant has a major impact on our daily lives.

It is a bit complex to explain how the Ascendant sign is calculated or determined, because it is not the position of a planet that determines it, but the sign that was rising on the eastern horizon at the time of your birth, as opposed to your sun sign, which depends on the precise time you were born.

Thanks to technology and the Universe today is easier than ever to know this information, of course if you know your birth time, or if you have an idea of the time but there is not a margin of more than hours, because there are many websites that make the calculation by entering the data, astro.com is one of them, but there is infinite.

This way, when you read your horoscope you can also read your Ascendant and know more personalized details, you will see that from now on if you do this your way of reading the horoscope will change and you will know why that Sagittarius is so modest and pessimistic if in fact they are so exaggerated and optimistic, and this is perhaps because he has a Capricorn Ascendant, or because that Scorpio colleague is always talking about everything, no doubt he has a Gemini Ascendant.

I am going to synthesize the characteristics of the different Ascendants, but this is also very general since these characteristics are modified by planets in conjunction with the Ascendant, planets aspecting the Ascendant, and the position of the ruler planet of the sign in the Ascendant.

For example, a person with an Aries Ascendant with its ruling planet, Mars, in Sagittarius will respond to the environment a little differently than another person, also with an Aries Ascendant, but whose Mars is in Scorpio.

Similarly, a person with a Pisces Ascendant who has Saturn conjunct him will "behave" differently than someone with a Pisces Ascendant who does not have that aspect.

All these factors modify the Ascendant, astrology is very complex, and horoscopes are not read or made with tarot cards, because astrology is not only an art but also a science.

It can be common to confuse these two practices, and this is because, although they are two totally different concepts, they have some points in common. One of these common points is based on their origin and is that both procedures have been known since ancient times.

They are also similar in the symbols they use, since both present ambiguous symbols that need to be interpreted, requiring specialized reading and training to know how to interpret these symbols.

There are thousands of differences, but one of the main ones is that while in tarot the symbols are perfectly understandable at first glance, being figurative cards, although it is necessary to know how to interpret them well, in astrology we observe an abstract system which is necessary to know previously to interpret them, and of course it must be said that, although we can recognize the tarot cards, anyone can not interpret them correctly.

Interpretation is also a difference between the two disciplines because while tarot does not have an exact time reference, since the cards are placed in time only thanks to the questions asked in the corresponding spread, astrology does refer to a specific position of the planets in history, and the interpretation systems used by both are diametrically opposed.

The astrological chart is the basis of astrology, and the most important aspect to make the prediction. The astrological chart must be perfectly elaborated for the reading to be successful and to learn more about the person.

To draw up a birth chart, it is necessary to know all the data about the birth of the person in question.

It must be known exactly, from the exact time it was delivered, to the place where it was done.

The position of the planets at the time of birth will reveal to the astrologer the points he needs to draw up the birth chart.

Astrology is not only about knowing your future, but also about knowing the important points of your existence, both present and past, to make better decisions to decide your future.

Astrology will help you to know yourself better, so that you can change the things that block you or enhance your qualities.

And if the astrological chart is the basis of astrology, the tarot reading is fundamental in the latter discipline. Like who makes you the astrological chart, the seer who makes you the tarot spread, will be the key to the success of your reading, so it is best to ask for tarot readers recommended, and although surely you cannot answer specifically to all the questions you ask yourself in your life, a correct reading of the tarot spread, and the cards that come out in the roll, will help guide you about the decisions you make in your life.

In summary, astrology, and tarot use symbolism, but the main question is how all this symbolism is interpreted.

truly a person who masters both techniques will undoubtedly be a great help to the people who will ask for advice.

Many astrologers combine both disciplines, and regular practice has taught me that both usually flow very well, providing an enriching component in all prediction issues, but they are not the same and you cannot do a horoscope with tarot cards, nor can you do a tarot reading with an astrological chart.

Ascendant in Leo

People with the Ascendant in the sign of Leo are the most optimistic of the zodiac, they know how to take advantage of the opportunities presented to them and can achieve any goal they set for themselves.

The Leo Ascendant has a need to show their individuality as well as express their creativity.

At times, this Ascendant thinks they should be treated like a king, since their ego is so big. They must do dynamic work to earn the status they think they deserve, and not get upset when they don't get what they want.

Their ego is strong and powerful, and they are theatrical and dramatic. These people must learn that when praise comes from the outside, they will never be completely happy or reach their full potential because these circumstances only serve to amplify their ego. People with Ascendant in Leo must learn to master their ego and if they want to succeed, they must focus on themselves, and not allow that vain side to take over.

Aries - Leo Ascendant

People with this Ascendant have a lot of enthusiasm. Aries and Leo are two fire signs, with a lot of potential, so they reinforce each other.

They are people with sky-high self-esteem, which is reflected in how others perceive them. They stand out for their kindness.

In the work area they excel because they are fighters, although sometimes they easily lose their temper. Their egocentric personality can interfere in their profession because they are dragged by their pride and the need to be the center of attention.

In love they are very sentimental, protective and, when they fall in love, they give their whole being.

Sometimes they are so vain and arrogant that they become toxic and controlling.

Taurus - Leo Ascendant

Taurus with Leo Ascendant lives in a constant quest for pleasure. This combination pursues success, both at work and personal level fiercely. They love status and prestige.

At work they make an active effort to succeed, and if they fail, they suffer great disappointment.

They are passionate and romantic, and love to court, but also to be courted. If they like someone, they will fight to win him or her over.

Its negative point is to splurge on luxuries.

Gemini - Leo Ascendant

Gemini with Leo Ascendant are very communicative people. They are always looking for new things to do and stand out for their versatility.

These people love to share and exchange ideas, so they tend to listen and value all arguments.

In the professional area they are interested in different branches, and they can succeed in any of them. The problem is the difficulty they have in concentrating.

In love, they are seductive people and have no difficulty in making friends. When they fall in love, they fight to be with that person and are committed to the end.

One negative thing about these people is that it can be easy for them to get carried away by their ego, belittling the opinions of others and trying to manipulate their thoughts.

Cancer - Leo Ascendant

People with this Ascendant are loving and family oriented. They possess much empathy and understanding and can genuinely help those in need.

They are idealistic and ambitious, so they plan many projects with optimism and succeed.

In love they are intense people and when they love someone, they are faithful.

This combination is a bit theatrical and sentimental which makes them magnify their emotions and turn even the smallest thing into tragedy.

Leo - Leo Ascendant

Leo with Leo Ascendant are people of great vitality, confident and who charm everyone they meet. They are leaders par excellence.

They are motivated at work, so they like to be publicly recognized, which motivates them to develop valuable skills.

They are optimistic and self-confident. They can face any challenge.

In the sentimental sphere they are very affectionate and protective. They crave recognition and value within the relationship. Sometimes they look more for someone who admires them than for a person who is in their own position.

Leo with Leo Ascendant are authoritarian and egocentric, especially if they have positions of power.

Virgo - Leo Ascendant

These people are generally not very thrifty, although they are not completely seduced by excesses. They have great ambitions and are very responsible for everything they do.

At work this combination is very resourceful and excels in their intellectual abilities. They are perfectionists and detest failure.

In love they are not so demanding in their relationships, but if they like a person they go out of their way to conquer him/her.

Libra - Ascendant Leo

Libra with Leo Ascendant are sociable by nature, accessible to everyone, which allows them to start relationships very easily.

This is one of the combinations that has balance. These people tend to be interested in learning intellectual subjects early in life.

In the sentimental area they are confident and determined, very passionate and socially gifted.

Scorpio - Leo Ascendant

This combination is of people who care about the welfare of their loved ones.

At work they have energy and strength to invest in their work. Normally they are ambitious people who are always looking for challenges and new ideas to apply. They fight to the end to achieve everything they set out to do.

They are conquerors, and nothing can stop them once they get someone or something in their head. They are totally devoted to their partner and need a life of intense sex and love to be comfortable in their relationship.

They are sometimes dictatorial, and do not usually listen to the opinions of others, nor do they listen to advice.

These people become obsessed and can destroy part of their life, work, and friendships.

Sagittarius - Leo Ascendant

Sagittarius with Leo Ascendant are kind and self-esteem people. They are affectionate and kind, they love to see others happy. They offer their protection to all their close circle and try to please because it comes from their heart.

They strive to find their true vocation. They are good communicators and excel in their multiple talents.

These people are very emotional, they love to love and be loved.

Sometimes these people are vain, sin of narcissism and get lost in the pleasures of life.

Capricorn - Leo Ascendant
Capricorns with Leo Ascendant are responsible people, they know how to manage life and everything around them. They possess a great willpower.

At work, they transmit conviction to those around them, and when they have a goal, they tend to achieve it. They have social skills and an eye for detail. If they use their resources correctly, they can achieve a recognized professional position.

In love they are charismatic, they like to be the boss in their relationships, becoming authoritarian, but they know how to recognize what is or is not reasonable.

Sometimes they can be overly critical and if they do not focus their qualities, they can sow chaos.

Aquarius - Leo Ascendant
Aquarius with Leo Ascendant are people who have strong ideals and love to transmit them. They are

people who know how to impose themselves and make others listen to their opinions with respect and admiration.

At work they like to excel and occupy important positions. They are altruistic, but they have an egocentric side that needs the recognition of others to be in balance.

In romantic relationships they seek good company and love to enjoy pleasures. Their ideal partner is one who is not submissive.

When someone obeys them, they lose their temper easily.

Pisces - Leo Ascendant

Pisces with Leo Ascendant are very empathetic, attractive, and seductive. They possess a great power of imagination and good intuition.

Professionally, they have an incredible nose for business, and their personal magnetism leads them to positions of responsibility and power easily.

In their relationships they can be a little selfish, but also altruistic with the people they love. However, with their partner they are attentive and generous.

They are prone to be vain and self-centered people. They seek attention at all costs, and this can cause them conflicts.

Saturn in Pisces, one of the most important astrological events.

March 7, 2023, was one of the most important days in that year's astrological calendar. Saturn, the stern teacher, and lord of karma, clashed with Pisces, the dreamer. This transit of Saturn in Pisces, which will last until February 2026, has not been a welcome mix.

Saturn is a planet of responsibility and strict authority, disciplining and structuring us as it transits through the zodiac. Saturn wants to make sure how we are achieving our goals, and when this planet moves through Pisces, the most spiritual sign, some important proposals are headed our way. Pluto and Saturn, shifting so in unison, will bring a gigantic energetic volcano, and guaranteed to be an unforgettable period. This may sound like a formula for battle, but this energetic combo can be effective and profitable.

Saturn is not satisfied in Pisces. It is difficult for him to found structures and build reality when everything is shifting. Pisces is a dual sign, so it can express itself in opposite ways; it can be both transcendental and practical. There is the possibility that Saturn in Pisces indicates the construction of forms above or below the water, or to dominate the water, such as pipelines, aqueducts, and ports. But it can also reveal the collapse of these structures due to hurricanes or structural fragility.

The Pisces archetype is contradictory to Saturn. It represents utopia, creativity, spirituality, and esotericism, as well as dreams, illusions, lies and escapism. It symbolizes the aspiration to flow like the sea, breaking down boundaries and restrictions.

The last transit of Saturn in Pisces was from May 1993 to April 1996, this stage saw the results of the collapse of the Soviet Union in 1989 which caused after-effects all over the world and crushed the Russian economy. Russia launched the first Chechen war in 1994 which lasted until 1996. The International Criminal Tribunal for the former Yugoslavia was established in The Hague in May 1993 to prosecute war crimes committed during the Yugoslav war in the early 1990s. On the other hand, the Bosnian war between Croats, Bosnians and Serbs spread with cruelties and ethnic cleansing, and various executions. The war ended in 1995, and most of the Bosnian Serb commanders were charged with genocide and crimes against humanity. In 1994 the Rwandan genocide began when Hutu gangs murdered more than 700,000 Tutsis, and untold numbers of women were raped during the massacre, which finally ended in July. The Iraq disarmament crisis, after the end of the first Gulf War, was at its height with much noise and no trust among those involved. A sect in Switzerland called the "Order of the Solar Temple" carried out a string of crimes and mass suicides, and here in the United States, Timothy McVeigh murdered 168 people in the Oklahoma City bombing. It was during this Saturn transit through Pisces that O.J. Simpson was arrested for the murder of his ex-wife and boyfriend, and released after a lengthy trial that was quite a Hollywood-style spectacle. In London, Fred West and his wife Rose were jailed after extractions in the backyard of their home of the bodies of multiple murder victims. South Africa had its first multiracial elections, and Nelson Mandela was elected president, later abolishing the death penalty in that country. Russia and China signed an agreement to stop provoking each other with their nuclear devices, and the Nuclear Non-Proliferation Treaty was endlessly amplified by 170 countries. In Australia, it was agreed to compensate indigenous people who were evicted during nuclear tests in the 1950s and 1960s.

Other events during the transit of Saturn in Pisces include religious currents, ideological movements such as socialism and leftism, the transmission of diseases and contagions, destructive behaviors induced by panic, an increase in the use of drugs and development of all types of art, as well as the means of maritime transportation.

Saturn in Pisces will see to it that we cannot use spirituality or fear to avoid certain conflicts that we must face. We can meditate, go to spend a hundred years in Tibet, and use the most powerful mantras in the universe, but at some point, we must also act.

During the last few years that Saturn has transited Aquarius, there has been a need to focus on individuality and being more genuine, rather than tolerating coercion from those around us. Although Aquarius is a sign known for dancing to its own beat, as Saturn is all about limitations, it has pushed us to sit alone with ourselves (remember the restrictions during the pandemic) and look at where we can place ourselves to create healthy boundaries.

All those lessons prepared us for what lies ahead with Saturn in Pisces. We will begin to be more sensible about how to add spirituality into our daily lives, while retaining an understanding of how to structure ourselves. Many people will abandon or question religions or dogmas.

Of course, there are many who will not savor this period, among them are religious guides and those who promote conspiracy theories. We will see conflicts between individuals of dissimilar religions, and many tendencies to try to dominate what others choose to believe. We need to accept that just because others disagree with our beliefs, it does not mean they are wrong. It simply indicates that their views are different, because at the end of the day, Pisces stands for inclusiveness. Something we lack.

As Pisces and Neptune rule the entertainment business, major studios and record companies will close, and many artists who have been connected to those studios will decide to create their own. If you are an artist, it will be in your interest to use your work beneficially, rather than letting the big companies at the top enjoy the dividends.

There will be less interest in special effects and a greater orientation toward self-contained films and themes that reflect the everyday. We will appreciate the beauty around us and be less motivated by glamour.

We often tend to see karma as something evil, but reaping what you sow is not bad if you have behaved well. Working with our karmic and subconscious baggage, understanding the past and being ready to let go, is decisive to manage this transit and come out of it successfully. If you dodge this, Saturn will punish you, but if you embrace it, you will arrive at a place that is predestined for something great.

Saturn's placement in our natal chart indicates where we are compelled to gain control of reality and assume greater responsibility. Pisces is the last sign of the zodiac, so Saturn's movement here also indicates an end or completion point for a much larger cycle.

Pisces is a water sign representing light, darkness, and the invisible worlds. It is known for its abstract ideas, and creativity. Pisces is mutable, which means it is adaptable, and open to the energies of the world around it. Saturn is a very solid energy. It rules over law, responsibilities and restrictions, and its energy can sometimes feel like a wake-up call, bringing us back to reality and making us face the consequences of our actions.

Saturn's presence in Pisces could feel a bit heavy because of all this, as the normally watery, intuitive, and sensitive Piscean energy will be forced to become a bit more reserved.

To understand it better you can think of it this way: if Pisces is smooth flowing water, the presence of Saturn is going to build dams, and these holds can direct the water in a productive and beneficial direction, but it can also feel more oppressive or controlling. However, there is a way to create a balance between these two energies, as the creative, intangible, and external ideas of Piscean energy can get some roots thanks to Saturn.

Saturn has a practical energy, so, if we combine this with the creativity of Pisces, there is a balance that can be achieved to help us take our creative ideas and bring them to life or even turn them into a business.

Pisces is also connected to religion and spirituality, so with Saturn there could be many questions around religion and spirituality and how it is connected to the rules that govern society, the spiritual industry may also get a wake-up call under this energy, or on a personal level your own attitudes and beliefs about your spiritual or religious connection will change.

Really what Saturn wants us to do is to step up and take responsibility for our lives and act in accordance with our authentic selves. Saturn may impose limits and restrictions that make us feel trapped or stifled, but this is only so that we can take the time to discover what we really want and what we are willing to stand for.

Below, you can read a synthesis of what the transit of Saturn in Pisces will bring for each zodiac sign. If you want to get more out of all this information, I recommend that you read the one for your Ascendant sign, if you know it, and then mix the interpretations.

Another way to get more information about this powerful planetary transit is to think about the themes that developed in your life the last time Saturn was in Pisces, which was from 1994 to 1996, to get additional information about what this cycle can bring you.

How will it affect the Leo Sign?

As Saturn transits Pisces, you may find yourself turning inward. There will be a strong pull to understand yourself on a deeper level and unlock hidden thought processes or subconscious patterns.

Saturn in Pisces can also bring a profound transformation of some kind in which you are guided to move through a process of death and rebirth.

Nature is constantly in a cycle of regeneration, trees lose their leaves, enter the phase of death and in spring, they sprout again, entering a phase of rebirth.

There is also the story of the Phoenix, rising from the ashes. You may find yourself taking a journey of death and rebirth with Saturn in Pisces.

You may need to clear a cycle or eliminate an outdated belief or lifestyle, and rebirth it into something new. Rebirthing an area of your life can always bring its challenges and with Saturn involved, there are bound to be challenges.

Saturn is like a strict teacher who will push you to be your best version. Saturn never pushes us too much or too little, he always seems to know just the right amount to bring out our full potential. As you move through this cycle of rebirth, you will reach a new limit of your potential.

You'll unlock new skills, travel to places you've never seen before, and ultimately come out of it all knowing yourself better and more intimately.

Saturn in Pisces is about getting to know the real you. It's about shedding the masks, the falsehood, the things that keep you stuck or limited, and peeling back the layers to reveal a truer version of yourself.

Saturn is closely connected with our soul contract; it is the contract we make before we arrive in this earthly realm. Our soul contract describes all the things that the soul is destined to learn and move through during its time in the earth school.

Saturn's job is to make sure we are living up to the tenants of our soul contract. He wants to make sure we are on the right path and doing what we are supposed to be doing, so anything that distracts us from our path will be removed and any karmic debts that need to be paid must be resolved.

Saturn in Pisces can also cause problems related to your sexuality and intimate relationships. You may need to reconnect with yourself and what brings you pleasure.

You may want to explore your sexual side or become more comfortable with your body. Saturn can also bring some boundaries and restrictions, so while you are ultimately encouraged to get to know yourself better and develop a deeper, more intimate relationship with yourself, you may feel the opposite at first.

You may feel disconnected from yourself and therefore disconnected from your desires and your pleasure center. You may be unsure of what you want from your intimate partners, or you may have difficulty communicating what feels good to you.

Saturn in Pisces is helping you to become intimate, but first you need to do this with yourself before you can do it with others.

Take the time to get to know yourself and what you desire, connect with what excites you, and perhaps work on your energy centers. Our lower chakras, which include your root chakra and sacral chakra, are located below the navel, and are connected to our feelings of security and our feeling of creative desire.

It is only when we feel safe in our own bodies that we can activate our pleasure centers. Therefore, find ways to feel safe and grounded in your own body, and it will be easier to return to a state of pleasure or joy.

It is possible that as Saturn moves through Pisces, you may need to rest, Saturn will guide you to take responsibility for your body and your mental health, it will encourage you to seek help if you need it.

Every time you are guided into a cycle of rebirth, there must also be some regeneration involved. You must give yourself the time and space to recharge your batteries to go through this cycle.

Just as trees remain dormant in the winter because they are preserving their energy, waiting for the right moment when the buds will blossom again. If trees never rested, they would not have the energy to form those new buds.

You need to give yourself equal opportunities and remember that all things will happen in due time.

Since you are a fire sign, you may feel the desire to rush, but Saturn in Pisces will teach your patience so that you can take your time and really consider why you are doing the things you are doing.

By the time Saturn finishes traversing this part of the cosmic heavens, you will feel more connected to who you are on an intimate level. You will feel more aligned with what brings you pleasure and how others can serve you, especially in your intimate relationships.

You are going to understand what you need to make sure what is no longer for you.

Saturn in Pisces is a bit of a challenging transit for you, and you will find yourself needing to close the door on something.

But remember, Saturn is there to bring you closer to your soul's path and a deeper state of harmony and understanding with what you want from your life. If you feel any challenges arising under this energy, come back to yourself. What do you really want? What feels right to you? You may not have all the answers, but whenever Saturn is involved, it's a good idea to return to responsibility.

Saturn wants us to take responsibility for ourselves and our lives. It wants us to take ownership of what we are putting out into the world and what we say we want. It wants to make sure that our conversation is aligned with our actions and that our thoughts are aligned with our soul.

Bibliography

Some information was extracted from the books published by the authors: Love for all Hearts, Money for all Pockets and Horoscope 2022 and 2024.

Articles written in the Nuevo Herald by one of the writers.

About the Authors

In addition to her astrological knowledge, Alina A. Rubi has an abundant professional education; she holds certifications in Psychology, Hypnosis, Reiki, Bioenergetic Crystal Healing, Angelic Healing, Dream Interpretation and is a Spiritual Instructor. Rubi has knowledge of Gemology, which she uses to program stones or minerals and turn them into powerful Amulets or Talismans of protection.

Rubi has a practical and results-oriented character, which has allowed her to have a special and integrative vision of several worlds, facilitating solutions to specific problems. Alina writes the Monthly Horoscopes for the website of the American Association of Astrologers; you can read them at www.astrologers.com. At this moment she writes a weekly column in the newspaper El Nuevo Herald on spiritual topics, published every Sunday in digital form and on Mondays in print. He also has a program and weekly Horoscope on the YouTube channel of this newspaper. Her Astrological Yearbook is published every year in the newspaper "Diario las Américas", under the column Rubi Astrologa.

Rubi has written several articles on astrology for the monthly publication "Today's Astrologer", has taught classes on Astrology, Tarot, Palm Reading, Crystal Healing, and Esotericism. She has weekly videos on esoteric topics on her YouTube channel: Rubi Astrologa. She had her own Astrology show broadcasted daily through Flamingo T.V., has been interviewed by several T.V. and radio programs, and every year she publishes her "Astrological Yearbook" with the horoscope sign by sign, and other interesting mystical topics.

She is the author of the books "Rice and Beans for the Soul" Part I, II, and III, a compilation of esoteric articles, published in English, Spanish, French, Italian and Portuguese. "Money for All Pockets", "Love for All Hearts", "Health for All Bodies", Astrological Yearbook 2021, Horoscope 2022, Rituals and Spells for Success in 2022, Spells and Secrets, Astrology Classes, Rituals and Charms 2024 and Chinese Horoscope 2024 are all available in five languages: English, Italian, French, Japanese and German.

Rubi speaks English and Spanish perfectly, combining all her talents and knowledge in her readings. She currently resides in Miami, Florida.

*For more information you can visit **the website** www.esoterismomagia.com*

Alina A. Rubi is the daughter of Alina Rubi. She is currently studying psychology at Florida International University.

Since she was a child, she has been interested in all metaphysical and esoteric subjects and has practiced astrology and Kabbalah since she was four years old. She has knowledge of Tarot, Reiki, and Gemology. She is not only the author, but also the editor, along with her sister Angeline A. Rubi, of all the books published by her and her mother.

*For more information, please contact her by email: **rubiediciones29@gmail.com***